WHY DO DOGS HEAR SOUNDS THAT HUMANS CAN'T? THE SCIENCE OF SOUND

CHILDREN'S SCIENCE OF LIGHT & SOUND

Speedy Publishing LLC

40 E. Main St. #1156

Newark, DE 19711

www.speedypublishing.com

Copyright 2017

IN THIS BOOK, WE'RE GOING TO TALK ABOUT WHY DOGS CAN HEAR SOUNDS THAT HUMANS CAN'T. SO, LET'S GET RIGHT TO IT!

WHEN YOUR PUPPY WAS FIRST BORN, HE COULDN'T HEAR AT ALL. HIS EAR CANALS WERE CLOSED AND IT TOOK ABOUT A WEEK FOR THEM TO OPEN. AFTER THAT, YOUR PUPPY WAS ALERT TO EVERY SOUND ALL AROUND HIM. YOU MIGHT BE SITTING IN THE LIVING ROOM QUIETLY READING A BOOK AND YOUR PUPPY IS HALF ASLEEP AT YOUR FEET.

SUDDENLY, YOUR PUPPY JUMPS UP AND STARTS BARKING, BUT AT THIS POINT YOU DON'T HEAR ANYTHING. THEN, ABOUT 30 SECONDS LATER YOU HEAR THE JINGLING OF KEYS IN THE FRONT DOOR. YOUR DAD JUST CAME HOME FROM WORK. YOUR PUPPY HEARD HIM COMING FROM OVER 80 FEET AWAY.

DOGS HAVE THE SAME SENSES AS HUMAN BEINGS DO. THEY CAN SEE WITH THEIR EYES, HEAR WITH THEIR EARS, SMELL WITH THEIR NOSES, TASTE WITH THEIR TONGUES, AND TOUCH WITH THEIR PAWS. DOGS DON'T HAVE THE BEST EYESIGHT BUT THEIR SENSE OF SMELL IS VERY WELL DEVELOPED.

I T'S THE BEST SENSE THEY HAVE, BUT SECOND TO SMELL IS THEIR SENSE OF HEARING. THEY HEAR THINGS IN THE ENVIRONMENT THAT HUMAN BEINGS ARE TOTALLY UNAWARE OF. OFTEN, DOGS CAN ALERT US TO DANGER BEFORE WE HEAR ANYTHING UNUSUAL.

HOW WELL DO HUMAN BEINGS HEAR?

SOUND IS CAUSED BY WAVES OF VIBRATION IN THE AIR. HUMANS CAN ONLY HEAR A CERTAIN RANGE OF SOUND VIBRATIONS. VIBRATIONS PER SECOND ARE MEASURED WITH A UNIT CALLED HERTZ AND ABBREVIATED AS HZ.

WHAT?

WE CAN HEAR ABOUT 20 VIBRATIONS PER SECOND OR 20 HZ AT THE VERY LOW END AND 20,000 VIBRATIONS OR 20,000 HZ PER SECOND AT THE HIGHEST END.

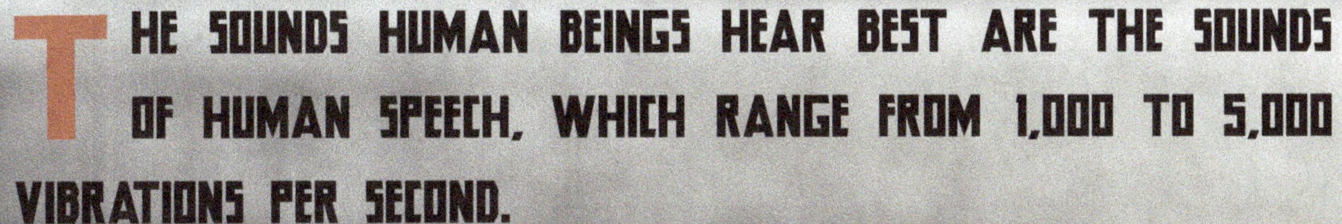

THE SOUNDS HUMAN BEINGS HEAR BEST ARE THE SOUNDS OF HUMAN SPEECH, WHICH RANGE FROM 1,000 TO 5,000 VIBRATIONS PER SECOND.

ALSO, AS PEOPLE GET OLDER THEIR HEARING ISN'T AS GOOD AS IT ONCE WAS. MANY ADULTS CAN'T HEAR MORE THAN 16,000 HZ. JUST BECAUSE WE CAN'T HEAR VIBRATIONS ABOVE THIS LEVEL DOESN'T MEAN THEY DON'T EXIST. COMMON HOUSEHOLD PETS, SUCH AS DOGS AND CATS, CAN HEAR MUCH BETTER THAN PEOPLE DO AND THERE ARE ALSO OCEAN CREATURES THAT CAN HEAR EVEN BETTER.

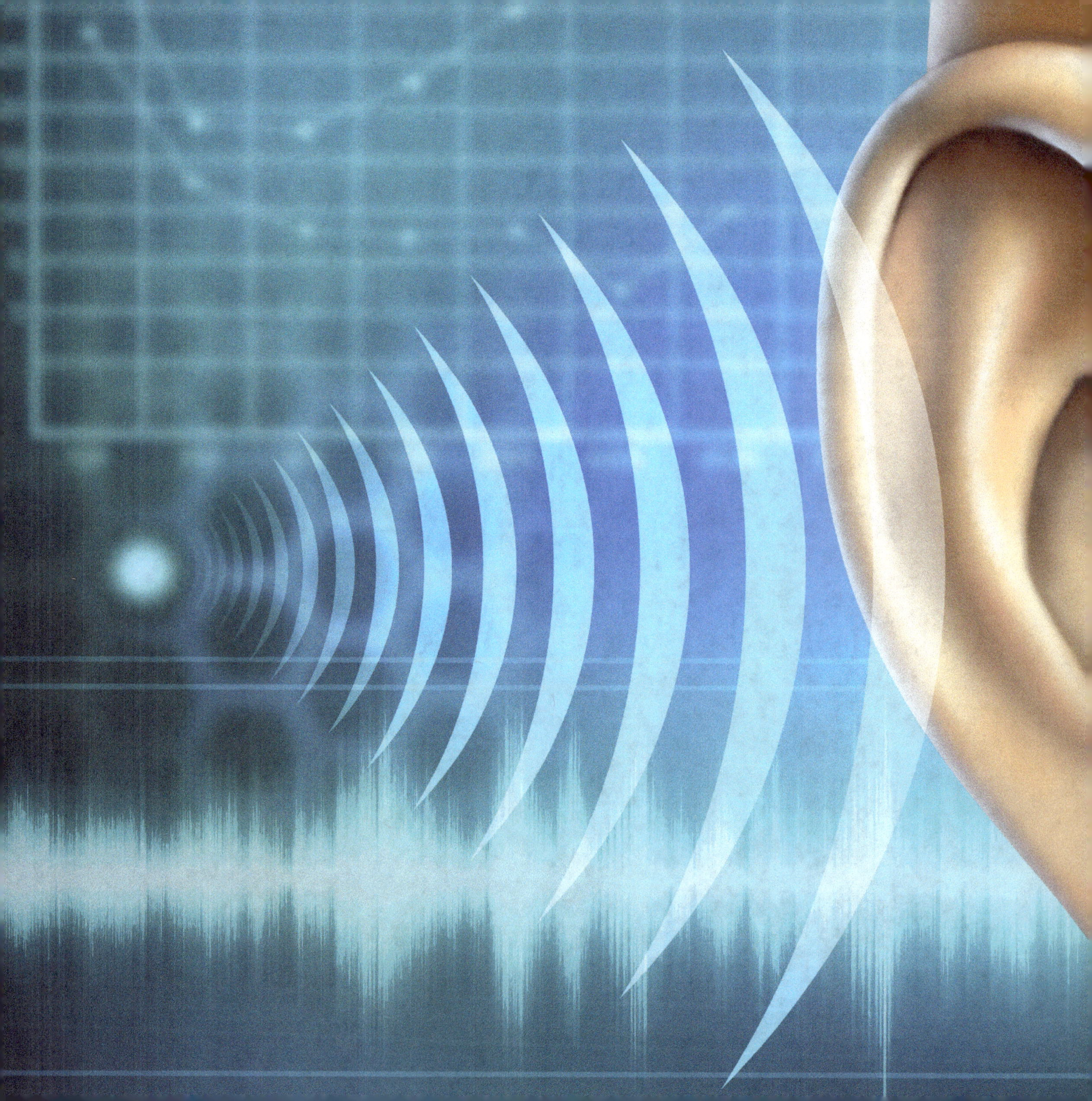

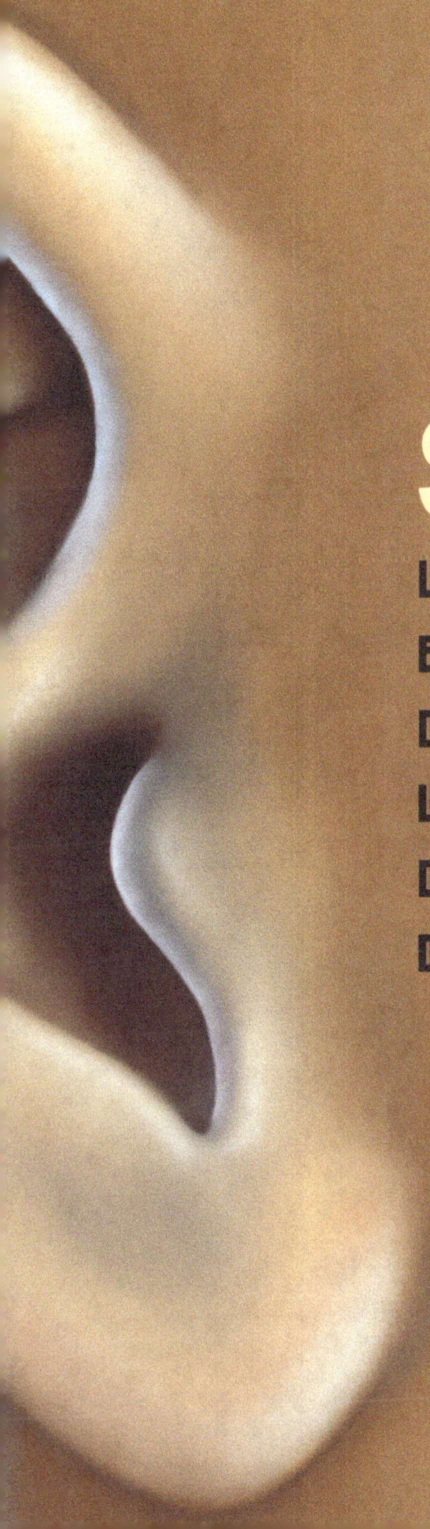

SOUNDS BELOW OUR HEARING RANGE ARE CALLED **INFRASOUNDS.** IT'S BELIEVED THAT ELEPHANTS USE INFRASOUND TO COMMUNICATE WITH OTHER ELEPHANTS UP TO 20 MILES AWAY. SOUNDS ABOVE OUR HEARING RANGE ARE CALLED ULTRASOUNDS. ULTRASOUND MACHINES ARE USED TO CREATE IMAGES OF THE ORGANS INSIDE OUR BODIES FOR MEDICAL DIAGNOSIS.

WHY DO DOGS HEAR BETTER THAN PEOPLE?

F YOU LOOK AT YOUR OWN EARS IN THE MIRROR, YOU'LL NOTICE THAT YOU REALLY CAN'T MOVE THEM VERY MUCH. YOU CAN MOVE MUSCLES IN YOUR FACE THAT WILL MAKE YOUR EARS MOVE, BUT THE 6 MUSCLES YOU HAVE IN EACH EAR AREN'T REALLY DESIGNED TO PIVOT YOUR EARS FOR BETTER HEARING.

On the other hand, your pet dog has 18 muscles in each of his ears! These muscles make it possible for him to tilt as well as rotate his ears almost like a satellite dish. With this amazing ability, he can adjust his ears to capture and funnel the sounds that he hears more effectively. Scientists believe that dogs tilt their heads for this purpose as well.

IN ADDITION TO THIS ABILITY TO FUNNEL SOUNDS, MANY TYPES OF DOGS HAVE EAR SHAPES THAT ACTUALLY HELP THEM TO MAKE THE SOUND LOUDER.

THAT MEANS THE SHAPES OF THEIR EARS ACT AS
AMPLIFIERS.

I T'S NOT JUST THE OUTER SHAPE OF THEIR EARS THAT HELPS DOGS HEAR BETTER THAN PEOPLE DO. THE STRUCTURE OF THEIR INNER EAR CANAL IS DIFFERENT THAN THE STRUCTURE WITHIN THE HUMAN EAR. THEIR EAR CANALS ARE LONGER AND THEY CAN FINELY TUNE THE POSITIONS OF THEIR EARS SO THEY CAN HEAR THE SOUND MORE PRECISELY.

THEY CAN ALSO HEAR THE SOUND FROM A MUCH FARTHER DISTANCE AWAY. IF WE CAN HEAR SOMETHING THAT'S HAPPENING 20 FEET AWAY, A DOG COULD HEAR THAT SAME NOISE IF IT WAS LOCATED AT 80 FEET AWAY. THIS IS WHY YOU MAY NOTICE THAT YOUR DOG'S EARS ARE PERKED UP AND SHE STARTS TO MOVE OR BARK WHEN YOU HAVEN'T HEARD ANYTHING AT ALL. MORE THAN LIKELY YOUR DOG HAS HEARD A NOISE FROM A VERY FAR DISTANCE AWAY.

HAVE YOU EVER HEARD A SOUND BUT COULDN'T TELL EXACTLY WHERE IT WAS COMING FROM? DOGS ARE SO GOOD AT HEARING THAT THEY CAN PINPOINT A SOUND'S LOCATION. IF YOU BLOW INTO A DOG WHISTLE, IT WILL MAKE SOUNDS IN THE 23,000 TO 54,000 HZ RANGE.

YOU WON'T BE ABLE TO HEAR IT, BUT YOUR DOG WILL BE ABLE TO AND WILL COME RUNNING. IN ADDITION TO HEARING THE SOUND, HE'LL BE ABLE TO PINPOINT YOUR EXACT LOCATION. DOGS CAN DISTINGUISH SIMILAR SOUNDS FROM EACH OTHER MORE EASILY THAN PEOPLE CAN TOO.

GUARD DOGS HAVE BEEN AROUND SINCE ANCIENT TIMES. BECAUSE DOGS CAN HEAR SO MUCH BETTER THAN HUMANS, THEY HELPED PEOPLE BY ALERTING THEM TO POTENTIAL DANGERS THAT THEY COULDN'T HEAR.

DOGS ARE USEFUL WHEN HERDING ANIMALS LIKE SHEEP SINCE THEIR TRAINERS CAN GET THE DOGS TO RESPOND TO SPECIFIC WHISTLES EVEN FROM FAR DISTANCES.

THE WORLD IS A PLACE THAT'S ALWAYS FULL OF NOISE WHEN YOU'RE A DOG. EVEN AT NIGHT, DOGS CAN HEAR THE PULSE OF THE INSIDE OF A DIGITAL CLOCK OR THE SOUNDS OF THE VIBRATIONS OF TERMITES AS THEY MOVE ABOUT IN THE WALLS OF THE HOUSE.

WHY DO DOGS HOWL AT SOUNDS?

SOMETIMES DOGS HOWL IF SOUNDS MAKE THEIR EARS HURT, BUT THIS ISN'T ALWAYS THE CASE. AT TIMES THEY HOWL BECAUSE THEY ASSOCIATE THE SOUND WITH SOMETHING ELSE. FOR EXAMPLE, IF YOU JINGLE YOUR KEYS OUTSIDE THE DOOR, YOUR DOG MAY HEAR YOU AND HOWL TO ANNOUNCE YOUR ARRIVAL.

SOMETIMES DOGS HOWL BECAUSE THEY THINK THEY HAVE CHASED SOMETHING AWAY BY BARKING. FOR EXAMPLE, IF YOUR DOG BARKS AT A PASSING AMBULANCE, HE MAY HOWL WHEN THE AMBULANCE RETREATS BECAUSE HE THINKS HIS BARKING MADE IT LEAVE!

DO DOGS EVER LOSE THEIR HEARING?

OLDER DOGS BEGIN TO LOSE THEIR HEARING JUST LIKE OLDER PEOPLE DO, SO A YOUNGER DOG WILL MAKE A BETTER GUARD DOG THAN AN OLDER DOG WILL.

DO DOGS SHOW EMOTIONS WITH THEIR EARS?

If you watch your dog you can tell if she's paying attention to you. If her ears are facing toward you, you'll know she's listening to the sounds you're making when you talk.

IF HER EARS ARE SLIGHTLY PULLED BACK, IT MEANS THAT SHE'S SHOWING YOU SHE'S FRIENDLY TO YOU AND YOUR FRIENDS. IF HER EARS ARE PRESSED AGAINST HER HEAD IT MEANS SHE'S SHY OR SHE'S AFRAID. YOU CAN TELL A LOT BY WATCHING YOUR DOG'S EARS. EACH OF YOUR DOG'S EARS CAN MOVE IN DIFFERENT DIRECTIONS TOO.

F YOU HAD AN X-RAY PICTURE OF THE INSIDE OF YOUR DOG'S EAR, YOU'D SEE THAT HER EAR CANAL TRAVELS VERTICALLY TOWARD HER JAW AND THEN MAKES A 45 DEGREE TURN IN A HORIZONTAL DIRECTION TOWARD THE EAR DRUM. THIS "L-SHAPED" EAR CANAL MAKES IT DIFFICULT FOR VETERINARIANS TO CHECK THE INSIDES OF A DOG'S EARS. IT ALSO MEANS THAT DOGS GET PARASITES AND INFECTIONS IN THEIR EARS FREQUENTLY.

ZOO BUS

ARE THERE ANIMALS THAT HEAR BETTER THAN DOGS?

DOG'S HEARING IS EXCEPTIONAL, BUT OTHER ANIMALS HEAR BETTER THAN THEY DO. A PET CAT HAS 30 MUSCLES IN EACH EAR AND CAN HEAR BETTER THAN A DOG. EVEN IF THEY ARE SITTING IN ANOTHER ROOM IN THE HOUSE, CATS CAN HEAR YOU OPEN THE CUPBOARD DOOR WHERE THEIR FOOD CANS ARE LOCATED.

WHALES AND DOLPHINS CAN HEAR SOUNDS THAT TRAVEL AT 100,000 HZ. AS A RESULT, THEY CAN MAKE SOUNDS TO COMMUNICATE OVER VAST OCEAN DISTANCES. THE PORPOISE HAS THE LARGEST KNOWN HEARING RANGE OF ANY ANIMAL. IT CAN HEAR SOUNDS FROM 75 HZ TO 130,000 HZ. MANY ANIMALS CAN'T HEAR SOUNDS IN THE LOWER RANGE.

White whale

THE RANGE OF HEARING IN DIFFERENT ANIMALS

HERE ARE SOME REPRESENTATIVE HEARING RANGES FOR DIFFERENT TYPES OF ANIMALS. JUST AS INDIVIDUAL PEOPLE DIFFER IN THE RANGE OF SOUNDS THEY CAN HEAR, SO DO ANIMALS SO THESE ARE JUST AVERAGE RANGES.

- HUMAN BEING, 20 HZ TO 20,000 HZ
- DOG, 50 HZ TO 46,000 HZ
- CAT, 30 HZ TO 50,000 HZ

- MOUSE, 1,000 HZ TO 100,000 HZ

- BAT, 3,000 HZ TO 120,000 HZ

- BELUGA WHALE, 1,000 HZ TO 123,000 HZ

- DOLPHIN, 1,000 HZ TO 130,000 HZ

- PORPOISE, 75 HZ TO 150,000 HZ

Porpoise

SUMMARY

Y OUR PET DOG CAN HEAR MUCH BETTER THAN YOU CAN. DOGS CAN HEAR SOUNDS FROM FOUR TIMES THE DISTANCE AWAY THAN PEOPLE CAN. DOGS HAVE EARS THAT CAN TILT AND ROTATE TO PINPOINT SPECIFIC SOUNDS AND THE EXACT LOCATION THE SOUNDS ARE COMING FROM. THEY CAN ALSO HEAR SOUNDS THAT VIBRATE MORE THAN TWICE AS FAST AS THE SOUNDS THAT PEOPLE CAN HEAR. MANY OTHER ANIMALS CAN HEAR BETTER THAN PEOPLE CAN TOO.

READ
THE
BOOKS

AWESOME! NOW YOU KNOW MORE ABOUT WHY DOGS CAN HEAR BETTER THAN PEOPLE DO. YOU CAN FIND MORE SCIENCE OF LIGHT & SOUND BOOKS FROM BABY PROFESSOR BY SEARCHING THE WEBSITE OF YOUR FAVORITE BOOK RETAILER.

Visit

BABY PROFESSOR
EDUCATION KIDS

www.BabyProfessorBooks.com
to download Free Baby Professor eBooks
and view our catalog of new and exciting
Children's Books

www.ingramcontent.com/pod-product-compliance
Lightning Source LLC
Chambersburg PA
CBHW081056140726
48009CB00014B/196